The Night When God Spoke French

The Night When God Spoke French

RAYMOND OLIVER

RESOURCE *Publications* • Eugene, Oregon

THE NIGHT WHEN GOD SPOKE FRENCH

Copyright © 2021 Raymond Oliver. All rights reserved. Except for brief quotations in critical publications or reviews, no part of this book may be reproduced in any manner without prior written permission from the publisher. Write: Permissions, Wipf and Stock Publishers, 199 W. 8th Ave., Suite 3, Eugene, OR 97401.

Resource Publications
An Imprint of Wipf and Stock Publishers
199 W. 8th Ave., Suite 3
Eugene, OR 97401

www.wipfandstock.com

PAPERBACK ISBN: 978-1-6667-1089-2
HARDCOVER ISBN: 978-1-6667-1090-8
EBOOK ISBN: 978-1-6667-1091-5

08/31/21

for Mary Anne, yet again

CONTENTS

Acknowledgments | xi
That Night | 1
On Dauphin Island | 2
"I Do" | 3
You | 4
To M.A. | 5
Reminder | 6
'Nuff Said | 7
Early Morning Spiderwebs | 8
On Anglo-Saxon Literature | 9
Dream Vision | 10
The Greatest Singer in the World | 11
Skipping Stones on a Lake | 12
Solidarity | 13
The Limits of Empathy | 14
To the Artist as a Young Child | 15
'Tis the Season | 16
Christmas Eve, 1999 | 17
Heavy Snowfall | 18
The Implications of Snowing | 19
"But speak the word only, and my soul shall be healed" | 20
"The Temptation of St. Anthony," Hieronymous Bosch | 21
On the Parapet of the Temple | 22
Birthday | 23

Words of Help | 24
Triptych | 25
Brother Roger of Taizé at Ninety | 26
Village in Winter, with Skaters | 27
Matters of Enlightened Taste | 28
Arriving | 29
Epigrams | 30
The Two Faiths | 35
Fall is for Long Journeys by Sea | 36
Photo of Church at Chapaize, Saône-et-Loire | 37
Church on the Hill (1805), Lenox, Mass. | 38
Authority | 39
Etymology | 40
Protests | 41
The Link | 42
A Contradiction in Terms? | 43
The Nature of the Confusion | 44
Time and God | 45
The Word "God" | 46
Snowdrifts | 47
Snow | 48
Ice Storm | 49
Now | 50
One Night | 51
Back in Lowell, Mass. | 52
A Share | 53
Already There and Always | 54
Preemptive Nostalgia | 55
A Little Theology | 56
Moviegoer-God? | 57
Our Worst Acts Point to God | 58
The Focus | 59

This Crowding In | 60
Chambord | 61
Noticing | 62
On the Overlook | 63
Introspection | 64
"I'll build a stairway ..." | 65
Triads | 66
Creation | 72
How It Is | 73
Andromeda | 74
One for Gabrielle de Coignard | 75
Life Modestly Heightened | 76
Edgar Degas, "The Dance Class," 1874 | 77
Through the Gate to the Domain | 78
On Reading Sixteenth-Century Verse | 79
The Plain Style | 80
New Notebook | 81
The Radio | 82
Being Remembered | 83
From Youth to Age | 84
My Will | 85
To My Grandmother | 86
Oct. 1, 2019, for Wil Mills | 87
Mardi Gras Float, Mobile | 88
The Atheist Disputed | 89
Soothing | 90
Loss | 91
New Year's Day, 2020 | 92
Postage Stamps, and Maps | 93
Bells | 95
Grasping | 96
The Four Last Things | 97

Preterition | 99
"Trouble in Paradise" on DVD | 100
Disappearing | 101
So Many Gone | 102
Through the Cancer Ward with Dr. Gottfried Benn | 103
On Jazz Funerals, New Orleans | 104
Choosing My Kind of Death | 105
Miss Katsura | 106
Also One of Us | 107
"Ce ne peut être que la fin du monde, en avançant" | 108
The Alfred Habegger Biography of Emily Dickinson | 109
Schöpfer | 110
Redeem: from Latin *redimere,* re-buy | 111

ACKNOWLEDGMENTS

Some of these poems and epigrams have appeared in chapbooks (Entries, Fireflies in an Old Yard, Other Times), anthologies (A Few Friends, A Garland for John Finlay, The Uncommon Touch), a previous book of poems (Raymond Oliver His Book of Hours), The Pushcart Prize 1983–84, and the following literary periodicals: Arizona Quarterly, Chicago Review, The Compass, Denver Quarterly, The Epigrammatist, The Greensboro Review, Hellas, Measure: A Review of Formal Poetry, Mississippi Review, Modern Age, The Southern Review, and TriQuarterly.

THAT NIGHT

We who proclaim that God is here (that's faith,
It's not like knowing "here I sprawl, in this chair")
Protest at times we're not well taken care of –
All those diseases, murders, accidents, wars.
But in a world where things are free to happen,
And we are free to will: we will, they happen.
When we open the window, bugs come in.
The luscious air, the world, and God, betray us?
No, they are doing what they do, like us.
As to God's grace, to recognize it look
Back, to those happenings that led you closer
To radiance, like that night at French House when
I met you. That was the night when God spoke French.

ON DAUPHIN ISLAND

For miles along the lucid beach
The Gulf of Mexico unrolls,
Piecemeal, in thin, illumined scrolls
Of surf, conveying ancient speech,

The message of the sea to land.
Its rhythm, colors, form, are clear
And it repeats. I overhear,
With love, and need not understand.

"I DO"

St. Paul's, Spring Hill, Fri. Aug. 28

Pews loosely full of teachers, family, friends,
With Patty at the organ up above;
As if to pledge a toast we promised love,
This morning where so much begins and ends.
We spoke two words—communion that we take,
Like that other with bread, wine, and "amen."

It was a sweet finality, as when
We fed each other chunks of wedding-cake;
Then honeymoon, first day our lives allowed
Together; then all those right up through now.

YOU

And are you like
A beam of light
Congealed, yet warm?
Like silence formed
To body? No;
However close
To truth, this "like"
Will always lie
A little. And you
Require truth.

TO M.A.

You are my own iconoclast.
When I, poetic solipsist,
Would make you over, you resist;
My faithless images you cast
Back in my face, till I can see
That you are there, amending me.

REMINDER

I've noticed that I don't
Like looking at you while
You're turning off the light
At night.
Mortality.

'NUFF SAID

A dream like poised remembrance of what might
Have happened: we had long been sharing time,
Then suddenly you had to leave; not flight,
Just being gone. Felt as wrong as a crime
Performed by God. I asked spontaneously,
As if proposing just a little tour
Around the garden, "Will you marry me?"
Quietly, casually, you answered "Sure."

EARLY MORNING SPIDERWEBS

Chissey-les-Mâcon

Thick mist, which hides the very hills
In vapid whitishness, distills
Its lucid droplets, to reveal,
In outlines that the half-light fills,
Designs that clear day will conceal.

ON ANGLO-SAXON LITERATURE

Once there were Angles, Saxons... What is left —
Splendid beyond the bits of gold, the wrecks
Of stone, a few fistfuls of twisted jewels,
The nave of Escomb Church, lonely and cool —
Are words, quick tracks of mind picked up on leaves
Of parchment, from which, still, their essence breathes.

DREAM VISION

If I could open only one of those days —
December 6, 1160, Oxford? —
Locked in the Mind where all our story stays,
What would I find? A high medieval quaintness?
Tall men at altars, mantled, stony-faced,
As in Autun's façade? Or men with eyes
Like goggles, limbs at funny angles, braced
To hurl their wavy spears, as at Bayeux,
In linen? Parchment peasants from the books,
In skirts and puttees, tending tiny sheep,
Gesturing statically with bishop's-crooks?

I see a snow-filled wood, not, as in Frost,
Lovely, but rough, indifferent, like Montana,
Part of the total frozen forest crossed
Only by fragile trails from far-off hamlets
To towns like Oxford there: no dreaming spires
But tufts of cottage-smoke in the early distance.
And here a clearing, where the morning fires
Reek of mere wood for heat, not roasting boar.
And from a thatched and earthy A-frame shack
A man comes forth, just for a moment pausing,
Smiling; in words like Dutch he hollers back
To make a woman laugh. I recognize him.

THE GREATEST SINGER IN THE WORLD

Caruso's train, on his Mexico tour,
Was stopped by bandits, who found out Enrico
Caruso was on board. They asked for music.
Was their leader Emiliano Zapata?
He might have known that only thing to do.

The singing brought such feeling-surge from solar
Plexus to eyes as the Virgin of Guadalupe
Might cause, raising a tiny child from the dead.
The bandits listened quietly, then left.

SKIPPING STONES ON A LAKE

The penny-slim
stone that spins
from his arched in-
dex finger skips
lightly in lit-
tle bumps, dip-
ping elastically
as far as we
think we can see —
then comes to rest,
sinking at last.

SOLIDARITY

for John and Dagmar

It isn't obvious that animals,
Looking at us, should look at not our feet
Or hands, for fear of blows, but at our eyes.
And in that mutual gaze or glance, we meet
As comrades in the quest for recognition.
No such meeting with rocks and trees. We mammals
Are all in this together, this soul-ambition.

THE LIMITS OF EMPATHY

A pair of crows almost as single crow
Silently cuddling on a telephone wire.
One of them separates by several crow-steps
And fluffs out wing like big feathery fan;
Pauses, flies off.
                      They have no grammar, though lots
Of signals. Unlike flowers, they have nerves
And must have feelings, if not love then fear
And needs. To watch them is like entering
An unknown force-field; only force is felt.

It feels like something to be crow.
But what that is, we cannot know.

TO THE ARTIST AS A YOUNG CHILD

You stand in swirling air and meditate
A look for your snowman's face. Of you remain
Traces of several minutes. Years are lost.

You shape him slowly, glancing up. You wait
For me, but cannot see me where I strain
Back from your future, which I slowly exhaust.

'TIS THE SEASON

To have a Holy Spirit consciousness
Is just the same as deeply wanting it.
Like when a wish for Christmas takes the form
Of bells and gifts and pine-scents being born
Within—before the fresh-bought tree appears — ,
Telling you Christmas is already here.

CHRISTMAS EVE, 1999

Here's Glühwein; take a swig,
In greeting to the Big
Turn, the millennium's!
The alcohol that hums,
Twanging my veins, expands
My heart with heat, commands
Benevolence to all —
"To all a good night!," I call,
Into the snowy dark,
To strike my little spark
Against the black, "and cheers
For the coming thousand years!"

Though we have merely drawn it,
This line in time, we're on it.

HEAVY SNOWFALL

Just let the lovely, whitely flickering air
Keep swiftly spilling down on everywhere!
I want this cold, distinguished outrage, snow,
To hide or trim the man-made things that show —
Vast concrete tumors, hand-placed boulder walls,
All is enchanted by the sky that falls,
This massive, crystalline invasion changing
The world; however often, still estranging.

THE IMPLICATIONS OF SNOWING

"Whose woods these are I think I know,"
Says Frost, while contemplating snow.
It's purity, austerity,
And quiet, that we treasure—we
Of old New England. It's those three
That falling flakes flawlessly show.

"BUT SPEAK THE WORD ONLY, AND MY SOUL SHALL BE HEALED"

I feel it in my solar plexus,
A tingling, sweet and piercing, gently
Opening out, as I begin
Thinking who exactly it is
That needs to do no more than speak
The word, for my soul to be healed.

"THE TEMPTATION OF ST. ANTHONY," HIERONYMOUS BOSCH

Grandfather, uncle, both were Anthony,
But I was named for a Spanish scholar-saint.
All temptations, unless politely faint,
Always threaten to be too much for me;
But that's the gist of tempting—just the threat,
The sheer appalling possibility.
(The scholar's caution helps; I'm deep in his debt).

Meanwhile, there are St. Anthony's temptations.
They're so eccentric! Is he relevant?
Black-cloaked he looks at us, his body bent,
Amid a chaos of hell-bent creations –
A demon-bird on skates, with funnel-hat,
Shrieking fish . . . not shaking his contemplations.
Tempting?? Not even the naked girl is that.

It's Bosch that's relevant, showing the grotesque,
Rightly seen through genius, as picturesque.

ON THE PARAPET OF THE TEMPLE

When with suicide Satan tempted him,
He wasn't next to Jesus but within,
Like heavy breathing. Satan drives the urge
To bad impulse, even over the verge
Of suicide or murder.
                      That's temptation:
Attack—not always causing occupation.

BIRTHDAY

Though Christ was born in 3 or 4 B.C. —
Before himself — we reckon him born in *aught*.
Though Arabs found the zero, it was he
Whose coming built an era on it; not
Some Caesar. What did Jesus do, to turn
His birthday to the bedrock for a tower
Of time? They say he gave us hope to earn,
With grace, freedom from time, its mortal power.

WORDS OF HELP

Auxilliary verbs like *has* and *is* and *will*
Are words that help us. *Has* is not possessive,
It signals past — pitiful has-been state,
Going nowhere, scentless like frozen life.
Is is the bursting on the scene, the stage,
Of something we are dying to see, as vibrant
With being as a cloudless western dawn.
Will is decisiveness, it rings with future,
Which in this setting has the color of hope.
"Christ has died, Christ is risen, Christ
Will come again." God helps us with these words.

TRIPTYCH

The Incarnation

He was stupendous light enclosed in clay —
So true to us, so easy to betray.

Stained Glass: the Crucifixion

Even on darkest days,
        Cathedral glass
Transfigures and displays;
        Like wine at mass,
It renders pain as praise.

"We have seen the Lord!"

Nonsense? But even fools know stone from bread.
The Christ they died for was alive, not dead.

BROTHER ROGER OF TAIZÉ AT NINETY

Your dying trumped all you had done before.
All your life you'd dazzled; now, even more.

Illuminata with her butcher knife
Went over to where you knelt and took your life,
There with your monks and evening's congregation
In your Church of the Reconciliation.

Intending with this act your perfect defeat,
She made your Imitating Christ complete.

VILLAGE IN WINTER, WITH SKATERS

The sundriness of twigs, fences, and cries
Is muted and composed by ice and snow,
Which, in their blank integrity, comprise
All wayward parts, making them darkly show.

The disarray is either edged in white —
Like bushes, branches, reeds, and window-sills —
Or smoothed, like yards and roofs. Blackbirds alight
Against the snow, whose cold decorum spills

Onto the ice-decked brook; there children, men,
And women, loud and fat as blackbirds, lurch
And skid, happily, resting now and then.
The ice blends with the sky and the little church.

That is their wholeness: being here, alive,
One country day in fifteen sixty-five.

MATTERS OF ENLIGHTENED TASTE

One of my kindly atheistic friends
Disputed what I called my Christian poems.
"Wrong as a divagation to Peking,"
He might have said. But let's suppose I truly
Had to go to Peking. Would he maintain
No one should do that? Like offering a proof
I had no business liking won ton soup?

ARRIVING

I don't like endless quest for God
As if the struggle, so courageous,
Were better than the having won it;
I'm no pioneer who prefers
The wrenching mountain-and-desert trek
To California's goldfields, prizing
The going there above arriving.

EPIGRAMS

In Sweden

They set a ring of nine stones in this grove;
And here, still, is thousands of years ago.

"I do not like thee, Doctor Fell"

I do not like thee, Doctor Death, thou fell
Teacher. I like whatever may dispel
Thy spell.—So, Christ, you cut with God's own knife
The bonds of death?
               I like Eternal Life
And want to bond with her, husband with wife.

Compacting

If we could take in hand the eloquent
And squeeze it down, it might be *elegant*.

A Poetics

Neither describe, narrate, nor talk — can verse
    Do anything the best of all?
Compactly, rhythmically in rhyme disburse
    Insights you will want to recall.

Confession

A little faith, a lot of hope, and not
Enough of charity. They're what I've got.

FAY ÇE QUE VOULDRAS

"And how am I by self-indulgence diminished?"
"Try It. You'll have the answer when you're finished."

Mary Dyer, Quaker Martyr, d.1660

Mary was killed by Christians for her love
Of Christ, which she proclaimed, this faithful dove.

At Valéry's Tomb

Le Cimetière marin, Sète

Eternal strikes the light through pines, while traffic
Moans in the vault of air. Where are you, now?

Incalculable

So many of us that have lived, then died!
Like galaxies of stars — but multiplied
By love and pain beyond the quantified.

A Distinction

So Graham Greene, "until today
Our greatest living novelist,"
Grew little, less, and shrank away.
Is this a ceasing to exist?
Nothingness? No, we *disappear*
Is all we know; less than we fear.

Aphorism

Whatever road our life may be,
Death is not its end;
It is a bend
Around which none can see.

Hear the Word

We need a word—say, "súivive";
The opposite of suicide.

Analogy

We are not God; God is not us; but when
We speak of God, while meaning what that's meant
To mean, that act reveals God is within.
(To speak of life, as such, presumes we've lived.)

Monkeys

Those of great faith believe that chance created
Reason, as in "monkeys enough, with time
Enough, could type out Shakespeare."
                                          Someone tried
The monkeys; quit when they couldn't even type
"A," which requires space on either side.

Conceptual Paradox

If mind is but the work of chance,
And "chance" a concept of the mind,
Daughter engenders mother: a dance
Of thoughtful atoms by chance designed.

Prayer for a Bureaucratic Foul-up

to a dear lady

If they assign us cancer, let it be
Prostate for you and uterine for me.

Her Moral Intelligence

for M.A.

You're the brightest person I've ever met.
If you don't get it, it's not there to get.

An Approach

To get at God, try to posit a State
Beyond defining, as far beyond as Mind
And Love and Beauty are from being weighed
On scales. You point towards God. You don't define.

THE TWO FAITHS

Death as final—annihilation—is
An article of faith in nothingness;
It's like that other faith in final life.
The one points eyes at such entire blackness
That seeing can no longer be imagined,
The other at a light so whole that seeing
Merely with eyes is as unthinkable
As fully hugging my wife with just my fingers.

FALL IS FOR LONG JOURNEYS BY SEA

Fall is for long journeys by sea,
To Europe and the festive past.
Not summer; heat and glare contrast
Too dully and obtrusively

With subtle, cool medieval tones.
October light, waning but clear,
Allows old values to appear
In church-glass, yellowed cloister-stones,

Or tapestries of love and war.
Crossing by sea is rough and slow,
Rightly: to leave the world we know,
For one that promises yet more,

We need the rites of passage. Fall,
Ripe time of change, fosters them all.

PHOTO OF CHURCH AT CHAPAIZE, SAÔNE-ET-LOIRE

Romanesque, from around the year one-thousand,
Of brownish stone in shapes angled or rounded,
The church is backed by hardest blue that frames
Its body and displays its point of aim:
Heaven. And high in the foreground: trees with black
Branches and spiderwebby twigs like cracks,
As if that great tower had pierced the sky
To scatter splinters of heaven far and wide.

CHURCH ON THE HILL
(1805), LENOX, MASS.

The church itself is white simplicity,
With huge black tower-clock, mortal reminder,
And tiny cross atop a cupola,
Reminding otherwise. Respective sizes
Of those two symbols tell us what has most
Room in our lives, but their respective heights
Tell us of value, like the massive weight
Of church organs compared to music they play.

AUTHORITY

Taking a sniff,
Getting a whiff,
Is how I'm liable –
For fear of swallowing
Too much, and wallowing –
To read the Bible.
Too deep and dense
For such as me,
But most importantly,
Too perilous. I must
Contend with its immense
Authority, and trust
(As if to read a risky medicine's label)
That I'll be set to follow it, and able.

ETYMOLOGY

This is our moral duty: *ecstasy*,
From *ex*, out of, and *histamai*, to place.
We must make sorties out of penned-in *me*,
To place us in the likewise penned-in *thee*.

" Love thy neighbor as thyself," by grace.

PROTESTS

in memory of George Floyd

We've seen tsunamis filmed: that vast advancing
Surge, implacable, wholly turning all
Humans have made, and humans, into rubble.
And now imagine a benign tsunami
Destroying vast, rotten structures of ours
And the perverted humanness that built them.
Not worth its price — George's murder. But
That's paid. At least let's have the cleaning up.

THE LINK

Is it a cobweb-filament, or clamp
Of steel, that links our politics with God?
The former, when it's ballyhoo and holy
Hullabaloo, the latter when it's values
Reaching down to the depths where they are made
And anchored, "ground of being" — thence to rise,
Like place to live in built to scrape the skies.

A CONTRADICTION IN TERMS?

John's wife of forty years, as beautiful
As sweet, and bright, and cherished, died at length,
Tortured, thus torturing her husband; died
From freedom. Freedom of her spinal cells
To turn cancerous, freedom absolute,
Right at the heart of this Creation (and note
The mitral valve in your old heart, which might
Freely stop working). Humans can be Hitler,
Microbes corona virus . . . God/Creator,
Lover of goodness, loves the choice of goodness,
But doesn't force that choice on freedom. Couldn't.

THE NATURE OF THE CONFUSION

Once, when I marked the terrifying teeth
And claws of Rabadash our charming cat,
Terror to littler beasts, I thought "How cruel
Of God to arrange such pain and death," since God
Created all. But no. In the beginning,
When that which did it, often hailed as God,
Said "Let there be . . . ", that was the all of it –
Sheer Being. Perfect act of love, like Rembrandt
Painting his portrait not from love of selfness,
But of the paint and canvas turned to vision,
To art — not predetermined servitude,
Like kiddie-train on track; only creation,
No wires attached. Freedom. And Love. (Confusing,
That free arranging we call "evolution.")

TIME AND GOD

We know that everything in the universe
Is caused, begins, and ends. No need to cite
Examples. Does the universe itself
End? Conceivable, poetically:
"And Universal Darkness buries All."
But that in which the universe exists —
Time? Like trying to imagine your fingers
Bending back to restrain their wrists: we can't
Conceive its starting or not, ending or not.
So it's outside the universe, contains it,
Somehow makes it, is always itself the same,
"Time" this abstraction, "God" not quite its name.

THE WORD "GOD"

Always the same, like ritual,
It opens with the back of tongue
On palate, closes with the tongue-tip
Above the upper teeth — describing
A horseshoe curve that moves my jaw
Down-up; repeating it, I feel
Like baby taking nipple-milk.
It doesn't name like other nouns;
What gives its meaning is a strangeness.
It is to words what human eyes,
Looking at you, are to the rest
Of all you'll ever look upon.

SNOWDRIFTS

Even with no "intelligent design"
Behind the fact of our intelligence,
Its works from Shakespeare to the hydrogen bomb;
Or behind nature, from the universe
To the electron (all of this the work
Of cunning falls of supernatural dice) —
Still we must grant to Random Antigod,
As we consider antic curves and peaks
Of snow like little moonlit palaces,
Artistic talent of the highest order.

SNOW

1

Once, in the hush before they sent the ploughs,
I saw the City all transformed: no crowds;
What had been filth, disorder, clanking, screaming,
Had put on such a form as Northern dreamers —
A Grieg, or Andersen, or Breughel — might
Have cast as spell, with art.
                              Beauty delights.
If Baudelaire can shape it from decay,
So can wind and snow from the everyday.

2

Snow is a blurring, white monotony?
But see those eaves and roofs highlighted, *see*
The wind-shaped swirls of air: variety.

ICE STORM

Look at the many shapes of twigs up there
Encased in ice, like icicles with backbone!
The palest glance of sun splendors them so,
You hear their glitter ringing in windless air.

NOW

Light goes a hundred eighty-six thousand miles
Per second: "one one-hundred, two one-hundred" –
In the time of saying eight syllables,
A piece of light has gone three hundred seventy-
two thousand miles. How many in a minute?
An hour? A year? In fifteen billion years?
(The moon is less than two such seconds away.)

Let's posit, fifteen billion light-years away,
The furthest end of the universe, a planet
Not unlike ours, in which a man and woman,
Much like us, are sitting reading, writing,
Or something like it, in this moment, right now.

I think their *now* and ours are the very same,
Identical exactly in their nowness
Just as my 3 pm Pacific time
Occurs the same moment as six in the east;
Different but same. It's not like occupying
Some specific space; space is stingy,
It won't let more than one entity in
At once, but *now* is generous; more than sunlight.
Infinitely. We're all in this together,
All being, in this unconditional *now*.

ONE NIGHT

They've lit their lanterns, people chatter, smoke
Drifts from the broiling fish, a woman scratches
Her ear—it's happening right now, just now,
But four hundred years ago in Edo, Japan.
Its contents change, but the nowness remains;
Like the act of breathing, always the same.

BACK IN LOWELL, MASS.

Saturday matinee at the Rialto,
Eleven cents, Laurel and Hardy, after
The colorless but loud newsreels of war
In Europe, bomb-blasts set to soothing roar
Of flying fortresses, with solemn newsman,
And martial music lifting us yet further.
Then Laurel, Hardy, manhandling large piano
Up six flights of stairs, on the fifth are told
The derrick's here at last; they turn and start
Manhandling it back down . . . Momently I
Am in those very instants. I've skirted time.

A SHARE

Is it a little touch of eternity,
A fingerprint upon a breath on cold
Glass, which will fade, but comes again at will? —
That changeless moment, say, of fascination
And shock from seeing Danny, when spaghetti
Kept coming from the bowl, put down the fork,
Grab with both hands, and tear the pasta apart
When I was seventeen. It's like a share
Of the eternal, because it's always there.

ALREADY THERE AND ALWAYS

Imagine that a memory of yours –
Say, putting in the mouth of Mary Anne
That piece of wedding cake—were not the mere
Image made of mist that it is for you,
But the real Mary Anne, hair short, eyes shut,
Mouth open, taking from your hand the cake.
That's how it is that she, and you, and all,
And everything, from start to finish of
The universe, are not remembered by
But present to the mind of God, always.

So we begin to see what heaven is.
We're embodied thoughts in the mind of God.

PREEMPTIVE NOSTALGIA

If winter shrinks, so all the fjords become
Miamis, as the sea (like population)
Rises, and Texas turns to jungle slum —
I will recall with joy my fingers numb,
Snow over all, and seasons in their station.

A LITTLE THEOLOGY

God's the essence of what we have within
At best — ability to reason, love,
Create. This God's the thereness of that there
Within, the causeless cause, which we can notice:
Like spending life in a daylit house, then one
Morning we look up and behold the sun.

MOVIEGOER-GOD?

Imagining a God not knowing all
That was, will be, and is, would be to flout
One's own imagination. Moviegoer-
God that wonders how it will all turn out?

OUR WORST ACTS POINT TO GOD

for my dear atheist friends

It may be that the God that you've rejected
Isn't the one that I've kept on accepting
Like urgent wine that graces daily dinner.
I'd found it makes more sense that we are sinners
Than sick or maladjusted or perverse,
Doing the things we do, which seem far worse
Than flouting man-made rules as of a game
That we've invented, which we have to play
So some of us, at least, can have a life.
These Dachau-deeds of ours aren't just "not right,"
They scream to the high heavens like the cries
Of tortured babies, these infinitely high
(Not crimes but) *sins*: offences of such a size,
Their trial needs that big God to preside.

THE FOCUS

So have I kept myself in mind,
Moment by moment, that I know
These changing selves not as a line
That graphs my progress young to old,
But as a focussing on and for
The world. It burns extremely here,
When I am mindful of my chore —
A consummation that appears
The less consumed as used and needed,
Like books that live through endless reading.

THIS CROWDING IN

This crowding in of what's uniquely mine –
This itching wrist, that bladder-urgency,
My thought of how you smile not parting lips,
The search, the finding of these words, whatever
Is most my own, like fingerprint of soul –
In its uniqueness is exactly like
The absolutely universal crowding
In of uniqueness on each conscious human.
We are all one, by our distinctive doings.

CHAMBORD

This largest of the Loire chateaux,
Small mountain's worth of weight in stone,
Distinguished corpse from France's past,
Cosmetically tricked out to pass
For quasi-living, comes alive —
Only, but extremely — in lines
Of wobbly brief memorial,
Incised in stone, like "St Michel
1699," "Donat
1772," "Legras
1834." I hear them,
Scratching their little lines and fearing
The lightness of their lives will make
No mark on time's adamant page.

It is their mark, and mine, I trace.

NOTICING

Not that I'm self-absorbed (although I am),
It's that this consciousness of self is all
I'll ever know of mind or soul or spirit
From the inside; as standing in a snowstorm,
Noticing, is the only way of knowing
What standing in a snowstorm's truly like.
So when we think of God, and want a hint
Of what God's like, carefully look within.

ON THE OVERLOOK

Ganesha Park, Pomona, CA

Acrid, medicinal, and fresh as the sea,
Those dusty eucalyptus leaves hang still
Above me; poems propped against my knee,
I too am propped, against the stripped and gleaming
Bone of the trunk. A clear pneumatic drill,

Above some mumbling freeway-sounds, ascends
Transmuted by the miles of golden air.
The city's at my feet; my vision ends
Only where haze takes over; I am twenty.
What are my prospects? How discern them? Where?

The terms, which I accept, are given, here:
Acrid, fresh, transmuted, stripped, and clear.

INTROSPECTION

Just spill it out like a bag of marbles, all
Colors, designs, and sizes, on a bed
So they won't roll—such contents of your head
(From chapters in your life) as you recall;
Pieces discrete as marbles, and as scattered.
Then play with them, and see what shapes emerge,
Setting in lines and curves both what had mattered
And hadn't much. Don't shirk the slightest urge
To find patterns.
                  It's hard, like using a knife
To carry marbles, this shaping of your life.

"I'LL BUILD A STAIRWAY . . ."

God existing but not
within would be as valid
as Alpha Centauri and
as relevant.
How then discern
divinity among the tangle
of oddments in us always
whispering or screaming
like a gifted but crazed
soprano "me-me-me-me-me!" ?
By noting that the problem
by being there
is already solved: hear
the word "God" in you; let
its implications unfold
like a majestic carpet leading
not down but up that celebrated
stairway to Paradise.
Listen.

TRIADS

Think About It

Through music, wine, and love, the world is stained
With wonder — which is truth,
Since what we are, and all, *truly is strange*.

Kindred

The Gothic cathedral and the redwood grove,
In high and ancient stillness,
In fragrances and shadows, stand alone.

Alfred Brendel Playing Beethoven's Piano Sonata in D major, Op. 28

They give a ring like yearning strong as fire
Yet crystalline, these notes,
These chords. Pure *sense of meaning*, at its highest.

The Chelmsford-Littleton Road to Perham's Cider Mill, 1946

Of faded asphalt, narrow, fitted to hills,
Patched like a leg of ancient
Dungarees, was the road to Perham's Mill.

Under the hand-cut beams, the cask dripped coldly.
Deep did I drink — and not of cider only.

The Traditional Jesuit

Salted by discipline, and smoked by doctrine,
Your soul's a Christian ham
So deeply cured that death will never rot it.

The Malcontent: Medieval vs. Modern

"Our faith was hunks of meat, tasty and juicy,
And nourishing! With gusto,
Like praying with our jaws, daily we chewed it.
From Christ Chrispies they feed us now, we're getting
Spirit-belches that taste like Diet Pepsi."

Bad Painting, Italian Renaissance

All glistening whitish, heaps of putti swarm,
Like large bowels, around
The Mother of God. Worship as puttiporn.

St. Gontran's Day, March 28

Poor Gontran. How's he feel, unknown, unprayed to?
Patron of victims, say,
Of chronic burping? He should be prayed for, maybe.

Walker Evans: Dustbowl Photo and Quotation

National Gallery

See what that woman's eyes have settled on?
Her dim horizon? *See it.*
("Die knowing something. You are not here long.")

Dog

Even abused, with mangy washboard ribs —
How good to be a dog!
He doesn't know he's going to die. He lives.

Fantasia

Desire, and memories of desire long cold,
Make us not wholly present.
Mostly en route, the heart — rarely at home.

A Free Moment

Today I noticed some shale with net-like cracks.

I need to cultivate
The quiet mind such quiet things attract.

A Couple

Two cats, curled up as one but set to leap
To life. Just right.
                I hope
We'll be together in eternity.

Reciprocity

Not that that smile I love is just a flash
To light your face; it says
My face has lighted yours. I treasure that.

My Wife Not Mother Tongue

Of fire and lucid air, its temperament,
In which "the dreadful sundry"
Of daily life sparkles. I speak of French.

No Boiled Spaghetti

Grasp your moments, their fullness, as intensely
As if with heavy pliers!
No *carpe diem* with fingers like spaghetti.

Reductive

Just meaty structures DNA has made
Of carbon, H^2O ...
Yes, but. We're chemicals with lots to say.

A Very Old Lady and the Christian God

Mindless, undone, she helplessly stinks. I feel
Humbled unto the ground,
That God prefers her to the likes of me.

Getting Older

The pages turned slowly, like Latin. Then
Slowly faster; and then
Faster less slowly ... someone's riffling them!

It Slips Me

"There is no time, just *now* with different scenes" —
I say this, know it, but
It slips me like the realness of my dreams.

Credo

A lifetime in a swing: truly believe,
Or faintly, in God, and how?

It might be better if God believed in me.

Combing My Hair

The universe beneath the hair I'm trying
To tidy needs, in turn,
A comb to tidy it — a very fine one.

CREATION

There was no time or space—duration, distance –
Before the making of the universe...
And part of space-time coming forth was us,
Like fleshy spirits charging out of the mist
When that great order was pronounced: "Exist!"

HOW IT IS

Imagine *now* as total energy,
Like particles of light, but everywhere;
Seizing on everything, like gravity;
Irradiating mind-stuff like the stare
Of God. Imagine, too, that its duration
Is infinitely brief, and that "before"
And "after" are just in our imagination;
And that this *now* keeps changing, evermore.

That's how it is, beyond the last disguise.
I can't imagine it as otherwise.

ANDROMEDA

for Miller McPherson

Skyful of stars was just a lasting scatter
Of sparks against the black; it didn't matter.
Then I heard that a tiny smudge of light,
Visible after gazing to the right
Off Cassiopeia, almost mere surmise,
Is the farthest thing we see with merely eyes;
That from these billions of stars, this galaxy,
The light took millions of years to get to me.

What matters is to know — like awe, like fear —
I've seen the inconceivable, right here.

ONE FOR GABRIELLE DE COIGNARD

She died in fifteen ninety-four; a poet,
Like me she feared her sometime-coming death,
And loved her right-now life. She showed both feelings
With words as fresh and right-now as my being
Alive right here. This means that my own life —
Urgent, precious, unique — in those three ways
Does not resemble but precisely is
Her life and that of the remotest humans,
Say a man of forty thousand B.C.
We're all as juicy, live, and fresh as any
Orange that's ever lived, however many.

LIFE MODESTLY HEIGHTENED

We walked ten miles to Kimball's Farm, and stopped.
A cone of black raspberry's what I got,
Lavender knob of smooth coolness, as tasty
As freshest roses rubbed in your nose are fragrant.

I'd made an icecream-memory at ten,
Walking so far. It was a Proust event,
Not on account of time remembered rightly,
But for the moment-seizing; time as heightened.

EDGAR DEGAS, "THE DANCE CLASS," 1874

The writer tells us what the painter gives –
Off-balance tiptoed arms-in-gesture girl,
One instant in the dancer's graceful whirl –,
And both attempt unerringly to seize
Existence from our fleeting world, to freeze
At least that moment, so it forever lives.

THROUGH THE GATE TO THE DOMAIN

Stone wall that crumbles, young with ivy, guards
A still December forest. Ice in shards,
On puddles, crackles cleanly under foot
The length of the avenue, on which they've put
Just patchy gravel; more a country lane,
But arched by lindens. This is the Domain
That I approach, glimpsing, through quiet snow,
Gables and chimneys of the small château.
Its very air is rich and private, scented
With slow, thick oak in a fireplace . . . Contented,
I dwell here in my self-beguiling mind,
With dreams that arise like twists of smoke entwined
With snow above that roof. The wished-for land,
Always within, imagined, at my command.

ON READING SIXTEENTH-CENTURY VERSE

After a while, sweetness begins to pall;
I seek plain herbs amid Petrarchan bowers.
For epigrams are weeds among the flowers,
Intruders in the garden since the Fall
Whose only pretense is medicinal.

THE PLAIN STYLE

Why the plain style? Why love simplicity?
Some books and paper, pencil, desk, and chair
Set in a little room, no room to spare –
All the necessities for one like me,
Beyond mere life-support. Why grasp for clutter?
I want just precious things that won't distract
My taste with hankering for sweets or fat;
Like eating real bread, and without the butter.

NEW NOTEBOOK

I touch this notebook with my pencil-tip
Like putting toes in cold fresh water; a bit
Exploratory, tentative, at first –
But then with growing need, even a thirst,
To get out further, deeper in the pond,
Exploring, moving, into and beyond.

THE RADIO

There is, has always been, something
steady and changeless within me, like
a radio tone that's audible
only when ads and programs halt
their seductive yammering,
briefly. It is clearly
the same in all
humans that are, have been, will be,
as clearly as that they
must take up space;
only the ads and programs
vary.
It is the sound
of Being.

BEING REMEMBERED

I think of all of you who've died,
Friends and family, one by one.
Is there a place where you abide
As in a drawer labeled "done"?

No, in a Mind where all's alive,
Where to be put is to survive.

FROM YOUTH TO AGE

1

We stay the same —
Yet not — as an arc,
Cast from a main
Of water, starts
Compact and small,
Then peaks, then down
Scattering falls
Unshaped to the ground.

2

The years, which here and there
Discreetly take a hair,
Muscle-fibre, or tooth,
Suddenly took my youth
And left in its place their fresh,
Unlovely pounds of flesh.

Outrage! But what to do?
— On journeys, watch the view.

MY WILL

If I can do
My will, as the blot
Of darkness spreads,
My last true thought
Will be of you.

TO MY GRANDMOTHER

Past ninety now, it is the night you dread,
Each night; you do not dare lie down in bed.
With your congested heart ready to break
You sit upright, trying to stay awake
In hope of dawn. Take courage; you are right.
To live indeed, fix your eyes on the light.

OCT. 1, 2019, FOR WIL MILLS

Today you would have lived for fifty years,
If you had not been stopped at forty-one.
Even more than your words, your face appears
Insistently to me. You were my son-
in-law, but also brother in the fight
To keep the old poetic forms alive,
The need to keep trying to say it right,
Plain truth in plain language, and not contrive
Sensational effects. Yours is the face
Of honest will not moving from its place.

MARDI GRAS FLOAT, MOBILE

Among azaleas in the night
Death and the Fool chase round and round,
One in black, the other crowned,
Their axis a Doric column.
They preach to Everyman who dies:
If life is folly in disguise,
Then death is foolishness outright;
So why be over-solemn?

THE ATHEIST DISPUTED

"Where are we after death? The same
Place as before our birth! Inane
Question." Except before our birth,
We hadn't existed; like a word
That hasn't yet been coined. But after
Dying—we've been. A different matter.

SOOTHING

My soporific comfort-thought
(Proudest achievement of the day,
To help me into sleep) was not
Of verse I'd written, but the way
I smoothly took the garbage out.
No insight needed; quickly begun,
No thought of what it's all about;
Clearly useful, and quickly done.

LOSS

Reviewing
years of my life
is like
riffling swiftly through
a thick book of pictures and text,
picking a word up here,
a number there, a face,
a snippet . . .
But this reminds me
that slowing down in life-
reviewing, to read
each page and wholly see
each picture, is not
an option.

NEW YEAR'S DAY, 2020

The youngish-looking one I'm used to being
Has nearly vanished; what I'm roughly seeing
Is my numerical future. But the rest?
My pathway toward the lost-at-last, or blessed?
It's not as certain as a decimal place –
It's the strange product of my will times grace.

POSTAGE STAMPS, AND MAPS

1

Glory and thanks! to printers for pretty stamps
With edges notched like battlements or lace —
My land of counterpane, by shaded lamps;
Better than Stevenson's, this play of place
With stamps so red-green-yellow-blue, as if
They'd picked up stains from where they're from. As bright
And new for me as its home, each stamp— so stiff
And sweet with glue I lick, absorbing right
Into my tongue the backs of colors Greece
Or Paraguay had pressed there. And designs!
I'd smell the Holland-scent their tulips make,
And feel the pointing snow, just tiny lines,
Of Fujiyama . . . And isosceles
From Tannu-Tuva, obsolete and long,
Weird as a fish they'd plucked from deepest seas.
New languages, new worlds where I belong!

2

Stamps are to album as maps to atlas — each
Collects a future, brightly out of reach
For now. Yet hoarded stamps, pledges of place,
Are charming, useless toys; but maps can trace,
Within a foot, those places. We consult

And wear out maps. Useful they are; adult.

I want whole albums' worth of futures that stay
Promising, fresh! and maps that show the way.

BELLS

What ails the "bells beyond the stars heard?"
Cast of the crystal of the spheres,
Perhaps they tinkled till they shattered.
Unless our ears, dull as our heads,
Only hear bells that ring like wood.

GRASPING

If death is nothing, if death *is not*,
How think of death, how think of thinking
Of death, except with handles — "ribs
As dry as feathers," "breathlessness,"
Or "depth without a breadth" — with handles
We make of words, with which we grasp
Nothing but handles, not the no-thing?

THE FOUR LAST THINGS

1 Death

Of death—our own, of those we love—we know
Our too-loved bodies rot like meat. We hope
L'interrupteur, that seems to turn us off –
That two-way switch—is interrupting not
The light but darkness. That it's turning us on.

2 Judgment

Our thoughts and words and deeds are as informed
With moral values as a tree with sap.
Value we don't invent, only its contents,
The yes-and-no ingredients of Judgment.
We tend them towards a flourishing—or other.

3 Heaven

"Rest eternal grant to him, O Lord:
And let your light perpetual shine upon him."
Yes, to imagine heaven, afterlife,
We must have images, or that belief
Will have the depth and value of the contents
Of a vacuum. But those two images
Are like an eternity in bed in Phoenix,
Next to a window full of sunlight never

Relieved by night.
                      Try this: we spend forever
With those we love, doing good things we do
On earth—but flawlessly, no helpless swerving
Into the selfish (now as nil as words
We've never heard). This isn't the famous "seeing
God," it's being caught up within God's being.

4 Hell

Must be the opposite of heaven—it's
Eternal pain, not life with God almighty,
Perfect pleasure. But logic calls for this:
Such an all-perfect Being could not rightly
Allow that hell, would be revealed as less
Than as defined. Let's call hell "nothingness."

p.s.

To hell
With hell.

PRETERITION

Those who called Calvin "the sadist of Geneva"
Forgot his doctrine of divine neglect:
God, not fiendishly torturing the damned
(Delighting, thus, the justified elect),
Just passed them over, like a choice God merely
Declined to make, not wanting to reject –
Like pushing from his nose the stench of sin –
But to bestow oblivion: *Forget*.

"TROUBLE IN PARADISE" ON DVD

Looking as live as if they were alive
(Not just the characters, the actors too),
They walk around in nineteen thirty-two
Burnished with youth, and in two thousand-five:
Kay Francis, Herbert Marshall, with flirting, fleeting
Beauty and wit, each hair and word in place,
Well oiled, and glinting by the tainted grace
Of bedlamps, costly venue of their meeting . . .
We freeze the frame. One of her smiles that burn,
While teasing, stops. This is the Grecian Urn.

DISAPPEARING

We'll go our way just like the fainter ones
In photos grave and stiff, lit by gone suns
(Our family, fading back); like them we'll go
Forward, with dot-dot-dot . . . to No one Knows.

SO MANY GONE

It's hard enough for anyone to face
Death. But imagine Shakespeare, with a world
Of people, actions, places in his head –
That stage on which all humankind took place,
In essence, like a brilliant storm that swirled
With order—thinking *he* must soon be dead!

THROUGH THE CANCER WARD
WITH DR. GOTTFRIED BENN

Necklace of tumors just below the skin:
"Palp them," says Gottfried. "Wages not of sin
But of our bodies, which begin to rot
In life a bit, and then, in death, a lot . . .
And here, this greenish oozing clump. Don't touch,
Just smell it. This is what we are. Not much."
Which is like seeing food, something delicious,
A shrimp and crabmeat salad, as the viscous
Mess in our mouth that it's about to be —
Or stomach-contents, from an autopsy.
He's brilliant, Benn, his poems what might come
From nectar-enemas up an angel's bum,
They're so sublimely, perfectly vile, eructive,
And fluent. Fine; but why so damned reductive?

ON JAZZ FUNERALS, NEW ORLEANS

"At birth we cry, because we're entering
A wicked world; at death we laugh and sing
Because we're leaving it.
                        We do not cry,
We dance to jazzy rhythms when we die."

CHOOSING MY KIND OF DEATH

More like explosion,
Or erosion?
Quickly done,
Or (painless!) spun
Out? Depends
On whether the end,
The slow one, is terror
Merely, or whether
They grant me patient
Fascination.

MISS KATSURA

I tend my young katsura tree, out front,
Since I enjoy her vegetable volition
To grow; she has no animal ambition
To kill; she stays rooted; she does not hunt.
So I dug her, thirty inches across,
A round of earth, with fertilizer packed
In mulch—some nutriments she might have lacked,
In tree-bark bits, with excremental sauce.
On this I weekly pour a little pool;
With winds and rain, that's all she knows of action.
She is a masterpiece of sweet inaction,
Mistress of peace to whom I go to school.
She teaches being. With her simple needs,
She carries on her life; and no one bleeds.

ALSO ONE OF US

Mornings, I throw my arms around Big Red,
The only redwood tree right at the sidewalk,
Only one I can lace my fingers around –
Little, for one so Big. The bark feels light
And soft; a touch of gentle in this giant.
Upwards, the branches radiate like spokes
Diminishing in thicknesses of green.
No language, no emotions or sensations
Because no nerves, no motion but for needles
And twigs in breezes, high above; yet life
So beautiful, so massive, has its rights.

> "CE NE PEUT ÊTRE QUE LA FIN
> DU MONDE, EN AVANÇANT"
>
> —Arthur Rimbaud

Aug. 2020, California

That tinge of smoke is like the scent of death
That distance gentrifies; it wets the eyes
A bit like sorrow. Sun is swollen, blurred
And orange. My morning walk feels ominous.

Thousands of lightning-strikes on grass and forests
Of tinder: nature striking up the band
To march us to perdition we have earned,
Heating the world with passion for our comfort
And money; the dance of death without the dancing.
"Could only be the end of the world, advancing."

THE ALFRED HABEGGER BIOGRAPHY OF EMILY DICKINSON

If she (from eighteen-thirty to 'eighty-six)
Could take up residence within my mind,
With her granitic father, drudging mother,
Ever more "pert" and sweet-lipped sister Vinnie,
Handsome seductive lively brother Austin,
Faithful Newfoundland Carlo, her flowers fresh
Or pressed, tiny poems in tinier script,
Passionate letters, baking bread, her friends . . .
All mixed with church, eternity, and God,
With ten below, Thanksgiving parties, death –
If she can live in me, well-nigh as present
As she was in her house on West Street, Amherst,
Then how much more must she, and you, and I,
All of us, live within that Mind we posit,
Not as in memory with its faintly seeing,
Hearing, but in the grip of total Being.

SCHÖPFER

"Immortality" is this word on paper
We use to praise the great ones, what they said,
Or did, or were. But *resurrection* is being
Remembered wholly, such that "being dead"
Is seen as nonsense (*is* is not?). That seeing
Is done by Am. Another name is Shaper.

REDEEM: FROM LATIN *REDIMERE,* RE-BUY

Just as I know, at night, exhausted, sleep
Will come, he knew, his rectal cancer having
Groped its way to his brain, that he must die.
I asked this firmly faithful Anglican priest,
"Any compensation in all of this?"
"No." He could feel no angel-feathers tickling
His hopefulness. He didn't feel it—but knew
He had a promise that his health, his self
Would be *redeemed,* in a buyback by the owner.

www.ingramcontent.com/pod-product-compliance
Lightning Source LLC
Chambersburg PA
CBHW060649150426
42813CB00052B/509